Mom, Can I Have My Long Hair Back?

Luisa Rodriguez Cantu
Illustrated by: Sierra Mon Ann Vidal

Copyright © 2016 by Luisa Rodriguez Cantu. 737877

ISBN: Softcover   978-1-5245-5235-0
       Harcover   978-1-5245-5850-5
       EBook   978-1-5245-5234-3

Print information available on the last page

Rev. date: 02/10/2017

To order additional copies of this book, contact:
Xlibris
1-888-795-4274
www.Xlibris.com
Orders@Xlibris.com

Dedication

To my children Joel, Regina,
and Aaron.
Thank you Kevin, and Freddie.

Special thanks to Mikael Samaniego-Lira for producing some of
the illustrations.

"Gibbons! Are you ready? It's time for your first haircut!" Mom yelled.

"Okay. I'm hurrying!" he shouted. Gibbons tiptoed down the hall from his room.

Mom watched and waited for him. "Oh, Gibbons," she sighed.

Mom grabbed the keys to the van and drove to the hair salon. Sister laughed out loud. His brother smirked.

"Gibbons, haircuts are not scary and don't hurt," she said.

"Yes, Mom. I'm okay with short hair for TODAY," he said.

Gibbons was quiet until he entered the salon. "Wow! I like this place!"

"Mom, can I sit on the dinosaur chair and the motorcycle chair?" Gibbons asked. Mom and Sister smiled. Everyone was glad to see Gibbons excited!

"Awesome! Gibbons let's walk around and see everything!" Brother said.

Miss Jackie, the hair stylist, showed Gibbons pictures of many haircuts.

"Gibbons, are you ready for your first haircut?" asked Miss Jackie.

"Yes, I am! I want my hair short TODAY and long hair TOMORROW," he said.

Gibbons eagerly climbed onto the dinosaur chair.

Everybody was surprised! Gibbons did great! He giggled while he listened to Miss Jackie's first haircut stories.

After Miss Jackie finished, the family gathered around his chair.

"Wow! Gibbons, I love your hair! Sport, you are ready for school." Mom said.

"Way to go, handsome!" Sister said.

Big brother smiled and gave him a high-five.

Gibbons looked at himself in the mirror.

"Wow! My hair is short! I like it Miss Jackie!" he said.

Miss Jackie hugged Gibbons and gave him a huge balloon.

The next day, Gibbons woke up and looked in the mirror.
He shouted, "Oh, no! Where is my long hair?" He ran from his room.
(Why did Gibbons run from his room?)

"Mom, I don't want my hair short TODAY!"

She said, "Calm down, Gibbons. Your hair will grow back, I promise."

"I can't play in short hair," he whined. Gibbons put both hands on his head and walked back to his room.

"I'm not going to school with short hair!" he shouted.

Gibbons stood upside down for a moment. "What am I going to do? Think. Think. I got it! I've got a towel idea!" he said. Gibbons ran from his room.

(What is a towel idea?)

"Surprise! Mom do you like my hair?" Gibbons asked.

"Tee-hee," she chuckled and said, "You funny boy. What is on your head?"

"I'm wearing long hair TODAY!" he said.

Gibbons wore a towel underneath his dinosaur cap. It covered his ears and neck.

"I will play in long hair TODAY, TOMORROW, and EVERYDAY!" he yelled.

Vroom! Vroom! He took off in his jeep.

The second day, Gibbons woke up and looked in the mirror. "Oh, no! Where is my long hair!" he shouted.

"Gibbons, your hair will grow back soon," Mom reminded him.

"Mom! I don't want my hair short TODAY!" he cried. "I can't play in short hair!" Gibbons sat in a large box.

"Think. Think. I got it! I've got a shirt idea!" he said with a grin.
(What is a shirt idea?)

"Ta-da! Mom, do you like my long hair?" he asked.

"Yes, Gibbons. I like your long hair." Mom smiled at him as she felt the long hair.

Gibbons wore a shirt underneath his dinosaur cap. His head peeked through the neck hole of the shirt. The shirt covered his ears and neck.

"Dinosaurs, I'm ready to roar! I will play in long hair TODAY, TOMORROW and EVERYDAY!" he yelled.

The third day, Gibbons woke up and looked in the mirror. He shouted, "Short hair again! Oh, no!" Gibbons ran from the room.
"Mom! I don't want my hair short TODAY!" he cried.
"Oh Sport, your hair will grow back." she said.

Gibbons walked back to his room. He rolled on the floor and wondered what to do next. "Think. Think. I got it! I've got a yarn idea!" he said. Gibbons galloped from his room.
(What is a yarn idea?)

"Hello! Mom, do you like my hair?" he asked.
Mom grinned and said, "I like your long, colorful, hair!" Gibbons wore long strands of colored yarn under his dinosaur cap.

25

The following day, was Gibbons first day of school. He woke up and looked in the mirror. He yelled, "Oh, no! Short hair again! I don't want to go to school! I want my hair long TODAY!" He slowly got ready for school.

Mom watched Gibbons as he walked from his room. He looked worried about his first day of school. She gave him a bear hug and said, "I love you, Sport."
She grabbed the keys to the van and drove to school.

Mom said, "Gibbons, you look handsome with your new clothes, new shoes, and new haircut. Miss Tommie Torres and your classroom friends are going to like your new look."
Gibbons said, "I can't play in short hair. Can I learn the alphabet, play Legos and work puzzles, in short hair?"
"Of course you can. Here we are," said Mom.

Gibbons walked quietly to his classroom.

"Hello. My name is Miss Tommie Torres. You must be Gibbons."
She smiled and greeted him.
Gibbons grinned and gave Miss Torres a high-five.

"Gibbons, our class will have breakfast in a few minutes." Miss
Tommie Torres showed Gibbons around the classroom. She said,
"Would you like to sit and work on puzzles while you wait?"

Gibbons looked for a table. He sat by himself and thought, *"Oh no. The kids are looking at me. I can't play or eat breakfast in short hair. What am I going to do? I want my hair long TODAY! I want to go home. I need my towel hair, my shirt hair, or my yarn hair."*

Suddenly, a little girl sat down by Gibbons.

"Hi! I'm Tamika. What is your name?"

"Gibbons," he said.

"Do you want to play?" she asked.

Gibbons was not sure what to say. He thought for a moment and said, "Okay. Yes. Legos and dinosaur puzzles are my favorites."

"I like to play with Legos and puzzles, too! Gibbons, I like your hair." Tamika giggled as she touched Gibbons' hair.

Gibbons had a fun first day at school. He whispered to himself, "Miss Torres and my classroom friends are COOL! I like school! I can work and play in short hair or long hair: TODAY, TOMORROW, and EVERYDAY!"

The End!

Printed in the United States
By Bookmasters